Out of Sight
Blind and Doing All Right

Out of Sight
Blind and Doing All Right

By Art Schreiber
As Told To Hal Simmons

Published by Nuevo Books
Los Ranchos, New Mexico

Printed in the U.S.A.
Book design by Paul Rhetts
Copy editing by Jill Ritz

Library of Congress Cataloging-in-Publication Data

Schreiber, Art.
    Out of sight : blind and doing all right / by Art Schreiber as told to Hal Simmons.
        pages cm
    ISBN 978-1-936745-11-1 (pbk. : alk. paper)
    1. Schreiber, Art. 2. Life change events. 3. Blindness. 4. Adjustment (Psychology) 5. Radio broadcasters--United States--Biography. I. Simmons, Hal, 1938- II. Title.
    BF637.L53S37 2014
    384.54092--dc23
    [B]
                                    2014016203

Photo of Art Schreiber on front cover © 2003 Carolyn Wright, Photographer, The Photography Studio, Santa Fe, New Mexico

Dedication

To my devoted wife, Alice, who helped me create my life and then didn't get to stay and enjoy it, and my children, Amy and Mark, who helped me get through the darkest hours into enough light that I could survive, and to Jeff.

OUT OF SIGHT: BLIND AND DOING ALL RIGHT

Acknowledgements

I wish to express my thanks for help I received in getting this book to print, not only from those whose names appear in the text and on the cover, but also from persons who read early drafts of *Out of Sight* and provided suggestions and encouragement on various aspects of the book. Those who assisted in advancing the work to completion in one manner or another include Melinda Walsh, Rick Walsh, Carol Scott Alley, Mary Jean Murphy, Greg Trapp, Kathleen Byrd, Ina Simmons, and Jill Ritz.

Hal Simmons and I became colleagues over a period of years when both of us attended meetings of the New Mexico Broadcasters Association Board of Directors. He is the author of two novels and worked as a journalist for several years.

In verbal storytelling, each time the story is told, invariably there are minor changes in wording and other details. Most of the stories in this book are based on my personal recollections of events that occurred in the past, and while I have tried to be as accurate as possible, there could be variations that others remember differently. *Out of Sight* represents my best recollections of the matters described.

Contents

CHAPTER 1
The Game Changer

Losing my eyesight was personally devastating.

I was fifty-four years old. The date was August 22, 1982.

The occurrence was unexpected.

It was the last day of a weeklong vacation for me, the first vacation since my arrival in New Mexico the prior year. At that time, I was general manager of radio station KOB-AM in Albuquerque, New Mexico. I had spent the last few days vacationing in Northern New Mexico with friends. My friends and I were staying at a first-class resort just north of Santa Fe, where movie stars often stayed while making movies in New Mexico.

That evening, following a meal at the resort's restaurant, I drove my car from the main lodge, where the restaurant was located, to my adobe condo just a stone's throw away. That was the last time I ever drove a car.

At the condo, I called the front desk and asked them for a wake-up call the next morning at six o'clock. I planned to spend the morning at the Indian Market Festival in Santa Fe before returning to Albuquerque. Shortly thereafter, I turned in for the evening.

As I lay in bed, I re-lived the past few days traveling in Northern New Mexico. We had visited fine restaurants, art galleries, and shops in Taos and had toured Taos Pueblo and the Taos Ski Valley just north of town. One of our stops had included the Rio Grande Gorge Bridge, which provided us with a high-altitude view of the scenic, wild river flowing far below. We had also spent an evening at the magnificent Santa Fe Opera.

Just before falling asleep at the resort, I remembered the fine meal and the service at the resort's restaurant that evening, the clear and cool high-mountain air, the bright stars, the soft glow of lights at the resort's lodge, the aroma of piñon and cedar trees, and the soft sounds of horses shuffling in the distance.

Life was good for me in New Mexico.

When the wake-up call rang the next morning, it all changed.

I fumbled with an outstretched hand to find the telephone receiver. It was so dark. "Why would the desk clerk be calling me in the middle of the night?" I wondered.

When I got hold of the receiver, the desk clerk said rather softly:

"It's 6 a.m."

"It can't be six o'clock," I thought. "Are all the curtains drawn? It's pitch black in here. Why is it so dark?"

I lay on my back in bed staring at where the ceiling should be. It was like I was back in that old swamp I used to visit near my home in Ohio when I was a kid. That swamp was near our family home, and at night, once I stepped inside the first row of trees, there was absolute darkness. Only the croaking of frogs and the chirping of crickets assured me I was still on planet earth and not lost in some make-believe place. This morning in the condo was like that swamp—so dark I couldn't see my hand up next to my nose.

Slowly a sense of unbelief, a sense of dread, and a sense of horror seeped into my mind. Could this be a bad dream? Or worse, could it be a bad reality?

Eyesight limitations were not new to me. But I had never experienced anything like this particular morning. Everything was black.

In early childhood, I lived on a farm and ranch operation about twelve miles west of East Liverpool, Ohio. My father was the minister at Madison Presbyterian Church. At one point, he was offered a job running a cattle operation during the day, not far from the church, to supplement his income. That started my life on a farm.

I was in the fifth grade at school when some of my personal habits finally attracted attention. One habit was holding my schoolbooks close to my nose when reading. Another was positioning myself in the front row of my classroom – there were only a half dozen students in my class level – so I could see the blackboard and the teaching cards held up by the teacher. My first eye exam resulted in a pair of glasses that had lenses so thick they looked like the glass in the bottom of soda drink bottles.

My school friends sometimes called me "Four-Eyes" and "Magoo." I didn't mind because for the first time I realized there were individual leaves on the trees and individual blades of grass growing in the ground.

With glasses I could function in a normal manner. That lasted until 1969 when I was forty-two years old.

One day I was attending a meeting of radio broadcast executives in San Francisco. Seated at a conference table with other executives, I became aware of a black dot floating in my right-eye vision. I blinked my eye several times and lightly rubbed it with my fingers, hoping that the problem would resolve itself and the black dot would go away. The black dot did not go away. As the meeting progressed, the black dot grew larger, eventually taking up half of the sight in my right eye.

I learned later that the black dot was the first symptom of a detached retina. Fortunately, my left eye was not affected.

In 1969, I was general manager of one of the strongest radio news stations in Los Angeles, KFWB-AM. I got immediate medical attention from a top ophthalmologist, Dr. Otto Jungschaffer. Unfortunately, my eye condition was difficult and complex. Efforts to re-attach my retina in my right eye were not successful. The retina would re-attach initially, but it would not hold. Then a staph infection gained a foothold, and then the retina held but the macula shifted position— at least that's how I understood it. As complexities mounted, Dr. Jungschaffer recommended I get a second eye evaluation from a leading retina specialist on the East Coast. I did get that evaluation, and it confirmed that Dr. Jungschaffer was doing all that could be done.

After the second evaluation, Dr. Jungschaffer recommended that since my left eye was doing well, we should leave my right eye alone for a while and keep it in reserve should anything happen to my good left eye. I concurred.

Prior to that recommendation, my days in the hospital in 1969 during the four surgeries had been long ones. I do recall one bright occasion when a well-known Hollywood movie star, Steve McQueen, dropped by my hospital room for a brief social call. He was a friend of my secretary at KFWB-AM, and he was interested in talking with me about some of my earlier radio reporting assignments involving other famous newsmakers.

On this particular visit, we barely got a chance to talk. Once word spread among the nurses that Steve McQueen was in my room, I suddenly started getting more medical attention than I had received in my whole life. There was a constant flow of hospital personnel in and out of my room. I was told later that outside my room there was a crowd of onlookers jockeying for a position to see the star when he departed.

When our brief visit ended, McQueen left me a publicity photo of himself, which I placed on a table against the wall. The next day the doctor told me I had to take the photo down. Too many nurses were coming into my room to gaze at it, causing disruptions in work routines. Thereafter, I posted the photo on the doorframe outside my room, and that solved the problem. I still have the picture to this day.

During the several months of surgeries in 1969, I continued as general manager of KFWB-AM Radio, doing most of my work over the telephone.

I also had to deal with episodes of substantial pain following some of the surgeries. The strain of continuing to work, even at a reduced pace, was an additional stress factor. That combination of factors put considerable stress on my family life with my wife, Alice, and my two children, Mark and Amy. Notwithstanding my edginess and freewheeling emotions, Alice helped me as I struggled through the whole period. When I worked to improve my depth perception by running up and down the spectator aisles at Drake Stadium on the UCLA campus, Alice was there with me. And when work pressures boiled, Alice was a calming presence who listened to my narrations of the day's events. I especially remember the stress of dealing with a labor strike and the day-to-day pressures of coordinating news coverage by KFWB-AM for headline news stories. At times, I was overbearing and close to irrational at home.

As years passed, I learned to navigate and function at home and at work using one eye. Eventually, there were only a few things I could not do after the loss of my right eye that I had been able to do before.

I continued my normal life's work as a radio station manager using one good eye until the day I got the wake-up call at the Santa Fe resort on August 22, 1982.

When I awoke that morning and realized something was grossly wrong, I soon concluded that what had been my good eye (my left eye) must have suffered a detached retina just as my right eye had a dozen years earlier in 1969. But now, in 1982, the situation was more shocking because I did not have an eye in reserve. For the first time in my life, both eyes were out of sight.

I remember lying there in bed thinking, "My God! My eyesight is gone."

CHAPTER 2
Some Help From Afar

On the same day I lost the vision in my left eye in Santa Fe, I made contact with Dr. Jungschaffer in Los Angeles. He said timing was crucial. He gave me the home telephone number of Dr. Robert W. Reidy, who he said was an outstanding ophthalmologist in Albuquerque. Unfortunately, it was Sunday, and it turned out Dr. Reidy was out of town. With the help of friends and my son Mark, I left for Los Angeles and met Dr. Jungschaffer in his office that same day. He operated on my left eye for a detached retina the next morning.

Over the next seven months, I was to have an additional ten surgeries on both eyes combined.

My left eye in 1982 was no more inclined to accept a re-attached retina than my right eye had been twelve years earlier. Finally, Dr. Jungschaffer suggested a new procedure that he thought might improve the vision in my right eye, the first eye to have lost retina connection. The procedure was not guaranteed, he said, but he thought it might work. We mutually agreed I would go for it. Another surgery was scheduled on my right eye immediately.

As long as I was in the hospital under the daily care of a nursing staff and Dr. Jungschaffer, my blindness was manageable. But as I lay in bed day after day, my thoughts began to surge towards the future: How was I going to survive when I got out of the hospital? How was I going to make a living? Would I be able to maintain my independence? How could I do anything if I could not see?

Following six or seven surgeries, I was more than willing to approve Dr. Jungschaffer's suggestion that I try a new procedure. As I lay in my hospital room awaiting transfer to the operating room just before the new procedure, I got a telephone call from Stanley S. Hubbard and his wife Karen H. Hubbard. Stan was president of Hubbard Broadcasting, Inc. in St. Paul, Minnesota, the company that owned KOB-AM in Albuquerque at that time. Despite my long absence, they had kept me employed and on the payroll at

KOB-AM ever since that night in Santa Fe. Stan said he and Karen were calling to wish me the best on this new surgery. "We're pulling for you," they said.

That particular call could not have come at a more crucial time in my life. While I hoped this latest surgery would work, Dr. Jungschaffer warned me that the procedure might not produce the desired results. I was worried. At the end of the phone call, Stan Hubbard said, "Remember, Schreiber, I hired you for your brains, not your eyes."

When I handed the telephone receiver back to my son, Mark, I told him what Stan had said. There was a long pause, and then Mark said, "Gee, dad. Wait 'til they find out your brain is gone too."

Results of Dr. Jungschaffer's surgery on my right eye to restore some light perception were touch-and-go for several months. Immediately after the surgery, I had no light perception improvement. Several months later, however, some incredible things happened. Mainly, some light perception began to return in that long-dormant right eye. Gradually, I recovered a portion of my right-eye vision. It was like looking out at the world through a drinking straw.

For many years thereafter, I saw through a pinhole in that right eye. At one time, my vision in that one eye was 20/80. Dr. Jungschaffer used to kid me by saying I could pass a driver's license test, but he also quipped, "If you do, let me know, so I can get off the road." He said this because I only had a 4 percent field of vision in that right eye. It meant I could read, but very slowly. While normal vision allows a person to read five to seven words at a time, I was lucky if I could see one word at a time.

During my last few months in Los Angeles, I stayed with my daughter, Amy, but eventually her work took her to San Francisco. My son, Mark, who recently had returned to Los Angeles, moved into Amy's house to help me.

For all practical purposes, I was legally blind. I still had my job at KOB-AM due to the generosity of Stan and Karen Hubbard. Since Mark had returned to Los Angeles, I continued to have non-stop family support.

I was living in a different world after August 22, 1982, in a new world I had never imagined. With vision in both eyes either gone or highly restricted, I told myself I had to go forward in life without the faintest idea of how I was going to do it.

CHAPTER 3
The Road Back

Since that morning at the resort near Santa Fe, I had been wondering how I could live without eyesight. In particular, making a living suddenly seemed beyond reach.

On the morning of August 22, when I woke up without my sight, I was staying in a first-class Santa Fe resort. I had driven myself there in a silver Mercedes Benz, furnished to me by my employer. I wore stylish clothes, lived in an upscale condo apartment, and enjoyed a steady income and prestige in the community, all of which were supported by my employment skills in a competitive broadcast industry. I had been with Hubbard Broadcasting only a couple of years and in Albuquerque just over one year—not long enough to have an extended network of longtime associates for support. How would I continue to do my job if I could not see, and where would I live if I could not work to generate income? My work skills outside of managing radio broadcast stations were limited.

For the first few weeks after my eyesight was gone, I thought my life was over.

I estimated that by using my financial savings, selling all my assets, and going on an austerity budget, I might last a couple of years before I was flat broke. All these thoughts flashed through my mind over and over again, sometimes changing, sometimes fading into the background, but always returning and threatening me with financial calamity and economic ruin.

It took me several months to block out the hopelessness of my economic situation. Eventually, I focused on the unfounded hope that somehow my eyesight would be restored. As long as I remained in the hospital under the round-the-clock care of the hospital staff and Dr. Jungschaffer, I could imagine my detached retinas being re-attached and my eyesight returning at some level. Initially, I believed the restoration of my eyesight was the one and only thing that would allow me to resume my career as it previously existed.

Many old friends in Los Angeles, my former residence, and a few more recently developed friends in Albuquerque gave me personal encouragement to struggle on.

Gradually, and without any basis other than faith and personal commitment, I decided that somehow I was going to find a way to work and survive. Somehow, I was going to resume my life. Somehow, I was going to keep going.

After an initial period of worrying about the worst economic scenario, I started thinking about the best economic scenario.

Looking again at my personal savings and limited personal assets, I concluded there was no way to replace cash flow except by returning to work. As a radio station manager, I had to stay in touch with a large network of people, ranging from employees to corporate supervisors, and from business owners to community leaders and social friends.

I had been hired to run KOB-AM as a power station, with fifty thousand watts of power—the highest radio broadcast power level allowed in the United States. It was my experience in the broadcast industry that once a fifty-thousand-watt radio station loses momentum, it is difficult to turn it around. Added to that concern, during the seven months I was away from KOB-AM, no one had held my position as general manager at the local level.

While I was in the hospital undergoing eye surgeries, my immediate supervisor was John Mayasich who was stationed in Minneapolis–St. Paul, Hubbard Broadcasting's home base. He was doing a first-class job of keeping the Albuquerque operation together. But without local leadership, the long-term prognosis for the station's growth was tenuous.

There were many days during my seven-month absence from work that I was not able to do anything. Even talking on the telephone was impossible due to medical treatments and regimens.

Perhaps the strangest thing of all was the fact that no one at Hubbard Broadcasting ever said anything to me about losing my job. Nor did anyone at Hubbard ask me about my plans should my employment end.

Instead, I just kept moving ahead with eye surgeries, and KOB-AM kept sending me my regular bi-weekly employee paychecks.

Finally, in March of 1983, seven months after the loss of my second eye, Dr. Jungschaffer raised the question of my returning to work. He noted that I had recovered some sight in my right eye (the first eye to suffer the detached retina) and that my medical condition was reaching a plateau. We discussed the requirements of my radio management position. Not long thereafter,

Dr. Jungschaffer gave me a green light to resume my work.

Thus in late March, I returned to New Mexico and to my job managing KOB-AM Radio. I was eager to see what I could do to help restore the station to a dominant position in the Albuquerque radio market.

CHAPTER 4
My Roots

My immediate passion to return to my broadcast job at KOB-AM was at the same level as my original passion had been when I was eight years old, listening to the radio with my father and dreaming of the day when that voice on the radio would be my voice.

My father, Valentine Adolphus Schreiber, was from a German family that lived in Meigs County, Ohio. His father (my grandfather) left home when my father was a child and to the best of my knowledge was never heard from again. My father was called "V. A." in family circles and among close friends and was an extraordinary person. He was taken out of school in the fourth grade by his grandfather, who was raising him, and set to work on a farm and in a blacksmith shop. At the age of nineteen, he left his grandfather's employ and took a job as a deckhand on a tugboat working the Ohio River. By that time, he was almost six foot four and weighed two hundred and fifty pounds. He was a powerful young man with a deep, commanding voice. In his early twenties, he left his work on the tugboat, which was stationed in East Liverpool, Ohio, about forty miles south of Pittsburgh, and got a job as a blacksmith. He not only shod horses to make a living, but he also repaired children's play equipment including sleds, bicycles, tri-cycles, roller skates and other toys, all at no charge. His physical strength, strong voice, and charitable nature made him a popular member of the community. He also was converted to Christianity by a charismatic evangelist preacher who was popular in those days.

While still living in East Liverpool, my father was encouraged to run for mayor on a ticket to clean up the local political corruption of the day. He did run, he did win, and he did clean up the town. When urged to run for re-election, however, he declined and instead joined the Anti-Saloon League to support enforcement of the national prohibition cause. He soon became Superintendent of the Ohio Anti-Saloon League.

About that time he married my mother, Nora Harrison, and they moved to Canton, Ohio. I was born in Canton in 1927. My mother was thirty-nine years old at the time. The first few years after I was born, my father was a person-of-interest to organized crime gangs in the area that supported alcohol sales and repeal of prohibition. A black limo used to park close to my parents' house, and men in dark suits watched our house day and night. My father carried a .38 caliber pistol. My mother didn't let me out of her sight for fear I would be kidnapped.

When prohibition was repealed during the Roosevelt Administration my father was out of a job; it was in the depths of the Great Depression. One day, three men approached my father and said they represented the Madison Presbyterian Church on Route 30 about twelve miles west of East Liverpool. They invited him to become the minister of that church, and he accepted. The pay was whatever was put into the collection plate, plus a house (without electricity or running water), and home-canned fruits and vegetables and live chickens left in gunnysacks in the church vestibule. For the first six years starting in 1933, the highest total donation on any one Sunday was three dollars and fifty-seven cents. A man who had been an adversary of my father on the prohibition issue purchased two thousand acres of land surrounding the church to start a farm and cattle operation. He invited my father to be the manager of the operation to supplement his meager income from the church. Soon we became a farming family as well as a preacher's family.

For many years, my father was not an ordained minister and could not perform church communions, marriages, and other church acts, but he was recognized as an outstanding preacher. His voice was one of his great strengths. He eventually was ordained during World War II, being one of a handful of people who were ordained without having a higher education or without attending seminary. The highest grade he attended was the fourth grade, but he was a voracious reader all his life.

My mother started her career as a telephone operator – a good job in those days – in East Liverpool. She eventually became a chief operator of the Ohio Bell Telephone Company. On a side adventure during the 1920's, prior to marrying my father, she moved to Albuquerque, New Mexico, and for three years worked as the chief operator at the Alvarado Hotel, a strange foreshadowing perhaps of my eventual move to Albuquerque over fifty years later. My mother was a good manager and handled most of the family financial matters.

When I was about eight years old, my dad would sit by the radio and listen to the news of the day. I began to sit with him during those radio programs. He did not encourage me to do that; I just loved listening to those voices coming over the airwaves. I soon decided that using my own voice on the radio was what I wanted to do. While no one spoke of it at the time, I did have a strong voice like my dad, and that gift would become the foundation of my career in radio broadcast news.

My transition to radio was slow in coming. It started when my speech teacher at East Liverpool High School asked me one day if I knew anything about football. Since I had played plenty of sandlot football growing up, I told her I knew something about it. Then she asked if I would announce the school football games over the stadium public address system. That was my start, and not long afterward, they asked me to do the basketball games as well. My love affair with a microphone had begun.

Upon graduating from high school, I enrolled at Westminster College, a United Presbyterian school in New Wilmington, Pennsylvania. I lasted only one semester, majoring in speech. Although World War II had just ended, I enlisted in the U.S. Army for two years, partly to serve and partly to qualify for the GI Bill, which would assure I could get all the way through college.

In the U.S. Army, I expressed an interest in radio operations, and they assigned me to the Signal Corps at Ft. Monmouth, New Jersey. My two-year army enlistment passed quickly, and after an honorable discharge, I returned to Westminster College. Financing my education was a challenge. While maintaining a full-time university schedule, I also worked as a hod (cement) carrier and became a magician with some hypnosis mixed in, thanks to extracurricular instruction by my German language professor. I learned seven magic tricks and put on shows in the community for which I received five dollars per show.

I also did some group hypnosis sessions for audience entertainment and for the entertainment of those who volunteered to be hypnotized. Usually, I would select ten people to come up on stage. I assumed I could get six of them on average to undergo some level of hypnosis, which was similar to going into some level of sleep or trance. On one occasion, I remember having a half-dozen people up on stage in a hypnotic mode. I told them they were at a horse-racing track and that they each were betting on a separate horse. I gave each person the name of his or her horse. Then I told them that when the race started they needed to shout loudly for their horse and that the louder they shouted, the faster their horse would run. There was a woman among them who was heavy set, not too tall, and who had a strong voice. Her horse was named Horacio. I announced, "They Are Off!" and then reported the progress of the horses around the track. My guests were shouting louder and louder as the horses neared the finish line with Horacio in the lead. "Go, Horacio! Go Horacio!" the woman shouted. When Horacio finished the race in first place, the woman was shouting and jumping up and down. Then suddenly, to my shock, she raced to the front of the stage and jumped off the edge, disappearing below. The stage was elevated about six feet above the lower level. I thought my goose was cooked! When I ran to the edge of the stage and looked down, I was amazed to see the woman still on her feet, in good condition, and ecstatic that her horse had won the race.

After my father's death during the World War II years, several elders at two Presbyterian churches where he preached asked me to fill in as the Sunday preacher until permanent pastor replacements were found. I did that for about six months.

Another job I did was waiting tables at the Alpha Sigma Phi Fraternity, which I had joined.

It was while attending a sorority-sponsored dance that I met a young woman named Alice Vogel. We became acquainted just before the Christmas holidays. After the holiday break, we arranged to meet each other at the student union building called the TUB, as soon as she returned to campus. At our designated rendezvous, I arrived early and got a table at the TUB. I had not been sitting there long when a stunning young freshman girl, whom I had never seen before, came by and sat at my table. It was such an unexpected pleasure that I struck up a conversation in no time. Unfortunately, some of Alice's sorority sisters were sitting at another table. They called Alice at her dormitory room and told her what was going on. The freshman girl left shortly thereafter, and Alice never showed. That was the end of our brief romantic encounter.

I later became the headwaiter at the girl's dormitory where Alice was staying. In that job, I tried flirting with her on every occasion, but she had started dating one of my fraternity brothers, and she wouldn't give me the time of day.

At the end of my second semester, my academic advisor called me in for a consultation and told me, "Arthur, you should get out of the speech department and get into something that will prepare you to make a living."

I was devastated. All I wanted to do was get into radio broadcasting. Instead of giving up speech, I added three other areas of study to my schedule including philosophy, psychology, and the Bible and kept going in speech as well. I also counseled with the head of the Psychology Department, and she told me not to follow the advice of my academic advisor but to follow my own dream, to work hard, and to get a job in radio. That is the direction I went.

During my senior year, I was sitting at a table in the TUB, and Alice Vogel walked by again. As always, I couldn't keep my eyes off of her. She was wearing a good-looking skirt and sweater, bobby sox, and saddle shoes. She also had the greatest figure.

Awkwardly, I jumped up as she passed by and asked her to join me. This time she accepted. I learned that she had broken up with my fraternity brother. That day I walked her to the sorority house, and we began dating right away.

A short time later, I "pinned" her. That meant I placed my fraternity pin on her sweater, and then the fraternity arranged a gathering in front of the sorority house where the brothers sang to us as we stood holding hands.

Things were moving forward in our relationship save for one major problem. Her parents did not like me. I learned later that they had been told that I was a ladies man and that I drank, smoked, and cursed. While there was some truth to that report, at the time I did not drink. That dry spell lasted until my second job in broadcasting.

Following graduation, Alice's parents sponsored her on a three-month trip to Europe, no doubt hoping the distance and time apart would cool off the romance. But Alice sent me letters and postcards during her entire trip.

Three months later when Alice returned to New York, her parents drove to pick her up. When they pulled into the driveway of their home in Mt. Lebanon, Pennsylvania, I was sitting on the front porch. I remember her mother's words: "Well, I guess there's no getting rid of him."

Alice took a job as an elementary school teacher in Columbus, Ohio, and I began interviewing for radio broadcast jobs in East Liverpool.

My first interview was at radio station WLIO-AM. I told the station manager I had no working experience in radio, but I wanted to be on the air. He gave me an audition, handing me some news copy to read. He operated the control room equipment.

When I finished reading the news copy, he came out of the control room and said, "Well, you were right."

I asked what he meant.

"You sure don't have any experience," he said.

Downhearted with that inauspicious start I walked down the street to a second radio station in East Liverpool, WOHI-AM. I did not know at the time that one of the station's announcers had quit and walked out just before I walked in the door. I met with the program director and told him I wanted a job. He asked me when I could start. I told him right now.

He didn't bother with an audition. He said the pay was thirty-five dollars a week. I told him the first station I talked to offered me forty dollars a week. He found that hard to believe but also said, "Ok. I'll pay you forty dollars."

By 1951, I decided to go to graduate school at Kent State to get a master's degree in psychology. My radio-station employer asked me to work at least on weekends, which I did, but it was a seventy-mile drive to do it. I finished my academic course work but never did submit a thesis and never got a master's degree.

Shortly thereafter, I returned to work at the radio station full time, re-committing myself to the world of radio news broadcasting.

Out of Sight: Blind and Doing All Right

CHAPTER 5
Changing Times

The radio experience I got at WOHI was of major value, and it confirmed that I was in the right career field. Within a short time, I heard of a radio station in Zanesville, Ohio, that was adding a television station to its operation. I applied for a job there. After an audition, they offered me seventy-five dollars a week. I was so shocked I wanted to jump over the manager's desk and give him a hug. Instead, I ran down the stairs and out onto the street looking for a pay phone. I spied the Zane Hotel, ran inside, found a pay phone, and called Alice in Columbus. "I'm making seventy-five dollars a week," I yelled into the phone. "We can get married."

We did get married in June 1953.

That job in Zanesville as an afternoon and nighttime announcer launched me on a new career track.

A working associate of mine in Zanesville got a broadcast job in Cleveland and later called me. He said the radio jobs there, in the big time, were no harder than in Zanesville.

Next stop, Cleveland!

I worked for six months at WERE-AM in Cleveland, where I was a newsman from three in the afternoon until eleven at night. I made less money than I had made in Zanesville, but I was promoted to news director in a short time.

It was during my time at WERE-AM that I got a news assignment to cover a young U.S. senator named John F. Kennedy, who was running for president in the Democratic primary election.

I traveled with Senator Jack Kennedy, his brother Robert F. Kennedy, and his wife Jacqueline Kennedy for several weeks through Wisconsin in the primary race against Hubert Humphrey.

Often when the candidate was trying to get as many media interviews as possible, we would pile into the same limousine along with Bobby Kennedy and Jackie Kennedy and race from one television station to another where Bobby would try to get Jack on a one-minute, live spot on the local television shows during the ten o'clock news.

During that campaign swing in Wisconsin, a typical day would start with an appearance at a factory entrance, with Jack Kennedy shaking hands with workers as they streamed in to start their day's work. Then it was off to restaurants for coffee breaks and shaking hands with every customer in the establishment. Luncheon speeches to civic groups followed and then back to new factory locations to catch workers on their way out the gates.

Often I would ride from place to place with the candidate, his wife, brother, and with three other national news reporters, who made up the full time news entourage. Jack Kennedy was easy to talk to, and he had a good sense of humor.

In looking back on the personal contact I had with the next president of the country, most of my attention is riveted to the tragedy of November 22, 1963, in Dallas. I was not on that trip. My next assignment on covering the Kennedy family after the assassination was at the rotunda in the United States Capitol in Washington D.C. The president's coffin was draped with an American flag. Jacqueline Kennedy arrived, accompanied by her two children, Ted Kennedy, Bobby Kennedy, and other Kennedy family members. There was a solemn atmosphere as Mrs. Kennedy and her young daughter approached the coffin hand in hand. When they reached the coffin draped with the American flag, Mrs. Kennedy and Caroline kneeled. A moment later Mrs. Kennedy leaned forward and kissed the flag.

I was live, on the air, describing the happenings, and I started to choke up. I was so emotionally merged with what was transpiring that my voice began to waver. Suddenly my producer back at the studio shouted through my earphones, "Send it back! Send it back!" Without thinking, I started to obey the order with a customary sign off phrase: "This is Ann Corrick with Art Schreiber in the Capitol Rotunda." Ann Corrick was a news colleague standing next to me. (I took a substantial ribbing when I got back to the studio for identifying myself as Ann.)

There were few dry eyes in that entire assembly of people watching the memorial.

Three years prior to the Kennedy memorial service, I had been approached by Westinghouse Broadcasting Company to switch to its radio station in Cleveland, KYW-AM. It was one of the major radio stations in the city at that time. Once again, I made a change.

News assignments from Westinghouse sometimes reached outside the Cleveland area. Shortly I was on my way to Alabama where I covered the civil rights strife in the South and the activities of Dr. Martin Luther King, Jr.

The civil rights protests stretched over several years through many of the southern states. My usual protocol was to fly into Atlanta, rent a car, and then join up with one of the marches.

Dr. Martin Luther King, Jr. sometimes would spend hours at his motel or hotel talking about the movement and his dreams and visions of racial equality. I attended these activities on numerous occasions. Dr. King was a moving orator whether the audience was a small congregation in a rural church or a mass gathering at the national mall in Washington D.C. On march-days, often I interviewed him several times a day, as would other news correspondents from national networks.

When the civil rights movement hit a quiet period, I was assigned to cover the tour of a group of young musicians from England who were making a splash and starting their first performance tour of the United States and Canada. They were the Beatles.

I missed the first few performances on the West Coast since I was covering the Democratic National Convention in Atlantic City. But as soon as the convention ended, I was off with the Beatles. I rode on the same chartered plane with them from concert to concert and stayed at the same hotels. Most often, they gave one performance and then moved on, but in a few places, they gave two performances, including the Indiana State Fair, Atlantic City, and Forest Hills in New York.

As a news broadcaster and reporter, my job was to travel with the tour and report on the Beatles' public appearances. I also got color stories from audience members, along with comments from the Beatles about their future plans and reactions to the tour crowds. Getting color stories was an easy assignment since so many people who saw the band members for the first time were awed by their music and live performance.

A performance usually began when Beatle support-staff members carried the band instruments onto the stage. The crowds became ecstatic when the band instruments arrived. When the Beatles appeared, it was pandemonium.

The normal arrival protocol started with three limousines arriving at the performance site. Crowds outside the entrance needed no warm-up act. The first limousine contained the Beatles. Security was waiting. The second limousine carried the public relations contingent and the stage manager. The news reporters, including myself, were in the third limousine. The crowds seemed intent on getting a chance to touch the performers, and since not everyone could touch one of the musicians, they settled for touching any one of the rest of us who were part of the entourage. During that tour, I had three suits torn to pieces by young, exuberant fans grabbing at me. I also lost two typewriters and three tape recorders. After a crowd encounter in Milwaukee, I discovered that someone had used a pair of scissors to cut off the inside portion of my necktie. One hotel where the Beatles stayed went so far as to take up the carpet from the Beatles' suite, cut the carpet into small squares, and then sell the squares as souvenirs.

Not long after the national political conventions ended and the Beatles headed back to England, Westinghouse asked me to move from Cleveland to Washington D.C. and become chief of Westinghouse's national and foreign radio news services. During my Washington D.C. tenure, we opened news bureaus in Paris, Madrid, Bonn, Tel Aviv, Rome, Copenhagen, Hong Kong, and Saigon. On each occasion, I would spend several weeks at the new bureau locations lining up correspondents. My annual budget allowance skyrocketed from about two hundred and fifty thousand dollars to about two million.

After several years as chief of the national and foreign news services, Westinghouse asked me to transfer again, to become general manager of KFWB-AM in Los Angeles, one of Westinghouse's top all-news operations.

While all of these career enhancements were exciting for me, our family's constant moves were stressful on Alice and our two children, Mark and Amy. We also had a third child, Jeff, who was born with cerebral palsy. The condition took his life less than two years later.

To add to our difficulties, Alice developed breast cancer in 1966 when we lived in Washington D.C. She had a right mastectomy that seemed to stem the cancer, and she enjoyed seven good years following that episode. Unfortunately, at Thanksgiving, in 1974, after we had moved to Los Angeles, Alice complained of some back pain. A medical exam showed that the cancer had returned and settled in her lungs and liver. The entire family was devastated. Her courageous battle with the disease ended seven months later. Alice had been the anchor for our small family. While I had worked outside the home to supply the income, she had taken care of so many family matters. Even at the last stage, she was suggesting items that needed to be done. During our twenty-two years of marriage, I had written only two checks. She had handled the entire domestic operation, just as my mother had.

In those days, Westinghouse moved its managers often, but due to extended personal difficulties and my 1969 eyesight fiasco when my right retina detached, they allowed me to remain in Los Angeles for almost eight years. Finally, in 1977, the word came down that they wanted me to move to New York City and manage their flagship station WINS-AM.

They gave me a lot of time to think about it. Neither of my children wanted to move.

Reluctantly, I finally made a trip to New York to look things over. During my brief stay there, I visited Alice's sister and her husband near Rochester. One afternoon, I took a walk alone in a wooded area on their property. While walking in that peaceful island of nature, I decided I could not make the move.

With some trepidation, I told my bosses I planned to stay in Los Angeles and would not be moving to WINS. It was a friendly parting, although they tried to talk me into reconsidering my decision.

For a couple of years after leaving Westinghouse, I worked as the president of Commuter Computer, a non-profit, public-spirited organization in Los Angeles that I had promoted and helped launch several years earlier while I was general manager of KFWB. Commuter Computer promoted carpooling and use of vans to get people to share rides to work. It was a successful program.

After two years with Commuter Computer, my heart was starting to feel a desire to return to my roots, radio broadcasting. About that time, an employment headhunter called me and said he had a client that was converting a rock and roll station into a news operation. "Any interest?" he asked. I told him I was not interested in returning to the Snow Belt, but he was persuasive and told me it was a beautiful area, without disclosing the exact location. In short, it was back to radio broadcasting for me. Stanley S. Hubbard eventually hired me to run KSTP-AM in Minneapolis–St. Paul, Minnesota. The day I arrived in the Twin Cities, the temperature was thirty-five degrees below zero. Even the Minnesota Vikings professional football team canceled practice that day. The temperature stayed at zero or below for the next month.

The next year, Stan Hubbard called me on a Friday while I was on a joint sales trip and visit with my children in California. He told me he would like me to move to Albuquerque and manage KOB-AM, a Hubbard Broadcasting-owned radio station there.

Without a second thought, I told him I was on my way and would be in Albuquerque on Monday. That was in 1981, less than a year before I was to lose the rest of my eyesight on that fateful night near Santa Fe.

CHAPTER 6
Back in the Saddle

And so the big day arrived for me in April 1983, when I made my first return appearance at KOB-AM studios after an absence of seven months for eye surgeries in Los Angeles. This was it. Could I run the same radio station I was running when the lights went out in Santa Fe? Or was this vocational return a false hope, an idealistic but unrealistic sentiment on my part? It was show time.

I enlisted the help of a friend to drive me to the radio studio. That friend got me to the front door. I pushed the door open and stepped inside. A receptionist at the front information desk greeted me and asked if she could help me. I realized at once that she did not know who I was nor did I recognize her since she was a new hire.

I introduced myself, told her I was the general manager of the station, and advised her I was heading to my office. It was down the hall corridor, take a left, then a right, and then use that pinhole of vision given me by Dr. Jungschaffer to find my office door.

Once inside, I looked around, knowing others had temporarily used my office during my absence. The desk drawers were cleaned out, and there was nothing on the desktop. My credenza was still in place. On the office walls, all of my framed personal photos remained, just as I had left them.

I purposely arrived early that morning to get my bearings before the building filled with people. Slowly, employees began to arrive. My first encounter was with some of the sales staff, whose office was adjacent to mine.

"Hi, Art. How are you doing?" they asked. No one mentioned my blindness.

Notwithstanding that obvious omission, I knew that my blindness and the staff's natural concern and curiosity about how my condition was going to affect my management needed to be openly discussed. Eventually, I decided the best approach was a group meeting of all employees to tell them my situation.

It was an expectant group of two dozen people that gathered in the studio's conference room.

I told them I was glad to be back, and I thanked them for keeping the station running during my absence. In a matter-of-fact manner, I told them I was legally blind, with only a tiny field of vision in my right eye.

"As we move along," I said, "if something about my blindness is bothering you, let's talk about it."

No one ever mentioned my blindness to me from that day forward.

The closest any person came to addressing my blindness may have been some time after my return. I was seated at my desk and was discussing a business issue with a person who was standing in the office doorway. As I was winding up the discussion, I noted that she had stuck her left thumb in her left ear and her right thumb in her right ear. Her palms were open and facing in my direction, and she was wiggling her fingers back and forth. Since my field-of-vision limitations required me to pan from one palm to the other, it took me a moment to realize what she was doing. Although this action surprised me, I did not let on. I wondered if she was jesting, telling me to go-fly-a-kite about the issue we were discussing, or if she was testing me. If I had responded, it would have told her that I did indeed have some vision remaining. If I did not respond, she would assume that I could not see what she was doing.

That minor incident did educate me that being a blind manager might affect some clients and employees in unexpected ways. It also underscored for me that I still could be an effective decision maker, but that things were going to be different.

While a major portion of my job was directing, unifying, and motivating KOB-AM's employees, I also had a significant role outside the station. I could not expect politicians, business and civic leaders, charitable-organization directors, and others to come to the station seeking me; I had to go out and seek them. Not long after my return, Hubbard Broadcasting added KOB-FM to my general manager responsibilities.

Typically, going to advertising agencies, government offices, business lunches, seminar sites, and committee meetings was the daily fare required of a radio station manager. With almost no vision, every trip for me was a new adventure.

One person who made a difference in my new life-without-sight was Fred Schroeder, head of the local affiliate of the National Federation of the Blind. Surprisingly, Fred's name came to me, not from a local source, but from a man named David Ticchi in Boston. Another friend of mine, who was working for a national, Sunday-morning TV program, called me one day while I still was in the hospital following an eye surgery in Los Angeles. That friend reported they had just done a show that featured a high-tech print-to-speech reading machine. He also gave my nurse the name and telephone number of a man in Boston who knew all about it—David Ticchi. I was excited that I might be able to access printed materials with the aid of advanced technology, so I called David Ticchi and told him that I was blind, that my friend was highly impressed with the reading device, and that I wanted to buy one. Ticchi was friendly and accommodating but began asking me details about how long I had been blind, what level of vision I had, and what training for the blind I had completed. His questions started irritating me. I told him I just wanted to buy the reading machine.

Ticchi then gave me the best advice I have received since losing my eyesight.

He told me I needed to learn to function as a blind man before getting a reading machine.

Upon reflection, I understood that advice to mean that when it comes to adapting your life to meet your own needs as a blind person, you have to pay your dues. This includes study, practice, acceptance of occasional failures, and the perseverance to learn the basic skills all blind people need to learn to function independently. Then you are ready and can utilize and benefit from the new technologies that enhance those basic skills. Ticchi asked me if I knew Fred Schroeder in Albuquerque. He told me that Fred, who also was blind, was the best white-cane travel man in the country. Ticchi's recommendation led me to Fred Schroeder.

Looking back, I now know there are few short cuts, and there are no magic bullets that take away the hard work of transitioning from normal vision to functioning without normal eyesight. Ticchi's advice put me on the right path to the realities of what lay ahead, and he gave me the name of the man who was going to lead the way. Ticchi's advice also gave me hope that things would get better.

Fred Schroeder played a major role in helping me learn what had to be done. He and a working associate, Sue Benbow, who is fully sighted, introduced me to a group of people belonging to the local chapter of the National Federation of the Blind in Albuquerque. I went to my first meeting with Fred and Sue, and they introduced me to a dozen people who were legally blind. Most of them were gainfully employed, and engaged in interesting social and family activities. They had the same inclination as everyone else to laugh and cry, rejoice and lament, and have emotional ups and downs.

Most of my alternative technique skills were learned under the auspices of the National Federation of the Blind. Fred and other members of the local chapter taught me by example that life does not end when blindness begins.

Out of Sight: Blind and Doing All Right

CHAPTER 7
Ups and Downs

During that seven-month period between my loss of vision in my left eye and my return to KOB-AM Radio, my mental and emotional life was topsy-turvy. The pendulum swung from hope of regaining my eyesight to mental depression over the possibility I might not regain any vision. There were down periods, when I lay helpless on a hospital bed for weeks, and a few up times, when I felt I was going to get back to work regardless of circumstance and despite what some people were telling me.

One medical provider who looked at my case told me I would never work again.

A nurse told me following a medical procedure that I was blind and "….you better get used to it, buster!"

On one occasion, I recalled the advice of that academic advisor in college who told me I should give up speech classes and study something that would help me make a living. Fortunately, I was able to tune out negative advice, both then and now.

In addition to the emotional roller coaster I experienced, I found myself exploding in anger when I tried to do some simple physical thing in a new way and failed.

Operating a telephone was something I had difficulty learning in the early stages. One day at my condo, while my son Mark was present, I tried to dial a local call and kept pushing the wrong numbered buttons. I tried one maneuver after another and couldn't reach the number I wanted. Suddenly in total frustration, I grabbed the phone and slung it across the room into the far wall, accompanied by some choice curse words. Mark retrieved the phone, which surprisingly was still in one piece, and put it back on the table.

In retrospect, using the telephone was not so difficult once a few alternative techniques were learned. One of those techniques required learning that on some phones there is a raised point or dash on the number five button about the size of a pinhead. Once your finger finds that pinhead on the number five button, the other buttons are not hard to locate.

I have experienced various kinds of anger, ranging from "Why did this condition happen to me?" to minor irritation over the way some people perceive a blind person. I also have talked to other blind persons who are angry at everything and everyone from their forefathers to God for their loss of vision. That is not a rare reaction, especially in the early stages of vision loss. Fortunately, it is a type of anger that dissipates over time in most people I have known.

Another irritation involves eating. When I am served at a restaurant, I have no idea where food is located on my plate. If you don't want to use your fingers to feel the food, the only other option is to gently probe around with a fork or knife and guess what is there by tasting. Peas are really hard to discern. Early on, I used to ask people sitting next to me where food was on the plate, but I prefer not doing that.

Two of my good friends in Albuquerque, who pulled about as many practical jokes on me as I did on them, kept my culinary life interesting. Jerry Danziger and David Herman, who ran KOB-TV in Albuquerque during my tenure with Hubbard Broadcasting, knew I did not like the twigs of green parsley that restaurants often put on plates. Once on an airline flight to Hubbard Broadcasting's home office in St. Paul, all three of us were traveling together. I had the window seat, David had the middle seat, and Jerry was on the aisle. A full lunch was served on a tray in those days. When I got my tray, I started probing around to locate the chicken, the mashed potatoes, a vegetable, and a roll. As I suspected, there were some twigs of parsley on the chicken. I carefully picked them off with my fingers and put them on the side of the tray.

With great stealth, Jerry and David walked up and down the plane aisle and solicited parsley from a number of the other passengers. They came back to our seating and started some light conversation. While I was distracted talking, David placed several parsley twigs he had collected on top of my chicken. When I realized there still was parsley on my meal, I carefully picked it off with my fingers a second time and set it on the side of my tray, as I had earlier. I assumed I had overlooked some parsley when I first removed it.

As soon as I placed a second group of parsley on the side of the tray, David replenished my chicken with another sprig. I started on the chicken again only to discover it was covered with parsley. We both repeated the procedure about four times before I smelled a rat. As the look of frustration rose in my face, David and Jerry couldn't keep from laughing. When I figured out what they were doing, I blasted them with a few choice words and eventually started laughing myself.

I should have suspected them even before they started laughing.

On another occasion, Jerry and I were at a seminar session of the New Mexico Broadcasters Association, where I was the seminar speaker. When my presentation ended, Jerry and I got ready to leave. "Art, it was a great talk," he told me, "but next time, face the audience."

David wasn't much better. Once, I was preparing to introduce the general manager of the local baseball franchise at a luncheon banquet. At that time, hand held portable phones had just made their debut, and I was fascinated with all cutting edge technology involving communications. I carried an early model that looked more like a shoe than the modern digital phones. I was seated at the head table next to David. When my time came to introduce the main speaker, I made my way to the podium, carrying my phone. Just as I reached the speaker's podium, my phone rang. I was addicted to it at that time, and it never occurred to me not to answer. In a low voice and as inconspicuously as possible, I answered the call. "Hello," I whispered. "Art," the caller said. I recognized the voice of my colleague, David, whom I had just left at the end of the table.

"Art!" he said again in his persuasive and inquisitive tone of voice.

"Yes?" I answered.

"Pass the butter!" David said.

Ever since my son Mark moved back to Los Angeles to take a job with a radio production company, I harbored a real fear about how I was going to make it without his being close at hand. During that period, I also missed Alice so much. When my first eye went out, she was a constant companion who continued to encourage me. Her death created a hole in my life I was not able to fill. And I was angry with myself for being a burden on my son and daughter. They had been the valuable bridge that got me over the first few months of totally lost vision. I don't know how I could have made it without their help during that crucial period.

Added to these feelings of anger and fear was the realization that there are a great number of pleasures a person has when they have normal vision which are taken for granted. At some point, I had to give up any hope I would ever experience those visual pleasures again. But, having grown up on a farm, I could still envision all those rows of corn growing in the fields, especially some of the ears that had multi-colored kernels. Then I would think of the rows of pumpkins and the jack-o-lanterns we would make from them. I would picture all the kids I knew who showed up in colorful Halloween costumes as we gathered for our trick-or-treat outings.

Fortunately, there are at least some minor trade-offs when vision is gone. The other senses do not get stronger, as some people imagine, but a person without vision does sharpen the sense of smell, hearing, touch, and even taste by relying on them more attentively. I became fairly adapt at recognizing people by their voices rather than their visual appearance.

A strange experience happened to me one day in October, just a few months after I returned to my job at KOB-AM. I had developed a physical fitness routine that included working out several days a week at a downtown Albuquerque health club. After finishing my workout on this particular day, I began my walk home along my customary route, west on Copper Street. When I reached the Sixth Street intersection, I crossed over and walked down the sidewalk parallel to the Immaculate Conception Catholic Church building. A narrow parkway area separated the curb and the sidewalk. A number of trees grew in the parkway. As I moved along the sidewalk, I could feel a layer of dead leaves on the surface. My white-cane tip stirred the leaves and a wonderful aroma of the fall season rose in the air around me. The smell brought on a sudden depression in me as I remembered the beautiful vistas of multicolored autumn leaves that I used to enjoy. I also remembered raking up piles of leaves around the farmyard and then running and jumping in the middle of them. That day, as I breathed the full aroma into my lungs, an invisible force pulled me off the sidewalk and onto the grass that grew in an area between the sidewalk and the side of the church building. An even thicker blanket of leaves covered the grass. As I veered off the sidewalk, I dropped my gym bag on the ground and lay my white cane down. At the same time, I fell down in the leaves and began vigorously rolling on them—first toward the church, then reversing and rolling back toward my gym bag. My face, hands, and sweat suit stirred up the leaves and moist grass as I rolled. "This is fall," I said to myself. "I can feel it. I can smell it."

As I rolled back and forth, my depression completely left me; I was exhilarated. A sense of peace, a love for the world, and a love of life filled me. "I can live," I told myself.

After a few moments, I rolled to a stop next to my gym bag. I grasped my cane and the bag, bounded to my feet, and resumed my walk home at a fast pace.

If any people were watching me during that rolling episode, they must have concluded I was drunk or crazy. In fact, I was neither. The aroma of fall had reached my inner spirit that day in some ineffable way that words cannot describe. The incident occurred over thirty years ago, and I still re-live that inexplicable feeling, especially in autumn.

CHAPTER 8
A Run for the Roses

At some point after vision loss, a person has to decide if they are going to change their lifestyle in order to stay in the game and stay active, or if they are going to throw in the towel and sit on the bench for the rest of their lives. Far too often, the message communicated by other people is that being blind means a person can't function in the everyday world. This negative opinion is a fallacy, a misconception, and a disservice to those who are blind or have low vision.

Not long after Dr. Jungschaffer's surgery miraculously gave me that pinhole of vision in my right eye in 1982, and while I still was recovering from the eye surgery in Los Angeles, friends helped me find the Services for the Blind Agency in California. The Agency offered training to help people like me who had suffered substantial loss of vision.

The training started with simple steps. In my first session, my instructor asked, "What can you do?"

"I can't do anything," I answered.

"Can you pour coffee?" she asked.

"I can't do anything," I repeated.

She produced a coffee cup and a Ping-Pong ball. "Place the Ping-Pong ball in the cup," she said. I did that.

"Now, take some cold water and slowly pour it in the cup," she continued, "and place the palm of your hand over a portion of the top of the cup." I did that.

"As soon as you feel the Ping-Pong ball touch the palm of your hand, stop pouring," she said. "You'll have a cup of coffee."

Then we repeated the process using warm water and then hot water and then coffee. One step at a time. After practicing, my instructor told me to discard the Ping-Pong ball and instead of the ball, put the index finger of my right hand (I pour with my left hand) inside the cup, so it touches the side of the cup. "When the tip of your finger feels the heat approaching, stop pouring," she said.

Before I left that first training session, when I learned to pour coffee, I had learned another important lesson: Many things people do when they have normal vision can still be done after a loss of vision, provided they are done in a different way. I poured coffee when I had close to normal vision; I can still pour coffee now that I have no vision at all. In training sessions for people who have lost their eyesight, this new way is called an "alternative technique."

I have remembered and used that key phrase "alternative technique" for over thirty years, and I am still learning new alternative techniques every year.

An alternative technique I had to learn quickly was how to brush my teeth. The problem was not so much that I couldn't use the toothbrush; it was getting the toothpaste on the brush before I put the brush in my mouth. The solution for that problem was to squeeze the toothpaste from the tube directly into my mouth and then insert the toothbrush. Simple but effective.

Little by little, I learned how to function during a normal day using alternative techniques. Each time I learned a new technique that helped me function independently, my confidence and motivation soared.

One of the most difficult skills I learned involved mobility and transportation. As mentioned earlier, my short drive from the Santa Fe resort's lodge and restaurant to my condo nearby was the last time I drove a car. Of all the challenges presented by a substantial loss of vision, the logistics of getting around— to home and work, to social events, to the doctor's office, to the grocery store, through an airport, and so on—are among the most complex. It is an issue faced not only by the blind but also by all persons who are disabled and prevented from driving or who cannot walk.

In brief, my solution to the mobility issues is simply an ongoing, daily effort to get transportation from friends and co-workers, to use public transportation at all levels, and to walk. I'll have more to say about mobility issues later.

The most basic solution for many day-to-day activities is to walk. Walking is a healthful, independent, and challenging activity.

I am a strong advocate of using a long, white cane. I have used white canes effectively for over thirty years. A white cane helps me detect and identify objects.

The use of a white cane does advertise that you are blind. That doesn't bother me. It does bother some people. For me the white cane is a valuable tool. It allows me to do things I couldn't do otherwise.

I was first introduced to white-cane skills by a man named Jose Sanchez, who was working for the New

Mexico Department of Vocational Rehabilitation in Albuquerque.

The first white cane training activity he showed me was to practice walking from my condo apartment in Albuquerque to my place of work at radio station KOB-AM— a distance of about seven blocks.

Jose Sanchez accompanied me on that route for several days to make sure I was accustomed to the trip. After a few days, he told me I was ready to solo and to practice the route on my own. He warned me not to get off course and not to go to any other locations during this early training stage.

That advice went in one ear and out the other. The first weekend after my training started, I needed to pick up some clothes from the cleaners. On Saturday afternoon, I left home and headed to the cleaners. It was only a couple of blocks from my condo but in the opposite direction from my work place. I made it to the cleaners, picked up my clothes in a plastic-bag covering, slung the clothes' bag over my shoulder, and confidently headed for home.

In the seven months I had been absent from Albuquerque getting eye surgeries, nothing had slowed down in the city. Across the street from the cleaners, a construction project was underway at a local school. Totally unbeknownst to me, a six-foot-deep, open trench had been dug between the sidewalk and the street curb along the school building. I moved fearlessly across the street reaching the curb with my white-cane tip out in front of me. I touched the cane on top of the curb and barely slowed down, expecting to reach the sidewalk in a couple of steps. Instead, I plunged head first into the six-foot-deep construction trench between the curb and the sidewalk.

I landed sideways in the bottom of the trench, which fortunately had some soft, wet dirt in the bottom. In that spot, I was out of sight in more ways than one. I yelled for help a number of times, but no one answered and no one came. After a wait, I decided I had to save myself if I was going to get out of the trench. I struggled to my feet, and after determining that I was not seriously hurt, I dug some holes in the soft earthen sides of the trench for steps. I threw my wet, muddied clothes bag and white cane up out of the trench. By reaching my arms up and over the top of the trench, I hoisted myself to the surface using my freshly dug foot holes as a base.

It is personally embarrassing and humiliating to fall into such a predicament even when it is understandable that such things happen, not only to the blind but to others as well.

I straggled back to the cleaners and stepped inside. The surprised clerk exclaimed, "Mr. Schreiber! Where have you been?"

"I've been in that damn hole over there for the past half hour," I replied.

"Please re-do my cleaning."

With loss of sight, there is no question that a person has to learn alternative techniques, use assistive technology, and undergo a change in lifestyle. But loss of vision does not equate with being unable to work, with being unable to socialize with other people, with not belonging to social and civic groups, or with not attending religious services or other public functions. And loss of vision does not equate with physical inactivity or being excessively dependent on others.

Staying connected to other people is of upmost importance since most people want to associate with other people and do things with others. It motivates us and helps us maintain a rational balance.

For me, staying connected meant returning to work, getting active in numerous civic and social organizations, working out in a physical fitness program, and learning how to navigate not only Albuquerque but other places as well, including Washington D.C., Los Angeles, Cleveland, and even other countries, including France and Mexico.

Not long after I returned to Albuquerque, I resumed working out at a health club downtown. One day I was talking to a friend named Molly Evanco, who worked out at the same club, and she told me it was time I got back to running. I told her that was impossible. Not in her opinion. Later we met at a running field, and she brought a piece of cotton rope about one foot long. She held one end of the rope with her right hand, and I held the other end with my left hand. In that manner, I was able to begin to run with her guidance.

Running always was one of my best exercises. After Molly got me going again, I volunteered to run in a 5K event. I was paired with U.S. Senator Jeff Bingaman of New Mexico who was an experienced runner. We didn't use a rope but Senator Bingaman made sure I was able to stay close to his side as we ran. He also provided plenty of conversation, so I could confirm I was staying on track. At the end of the race, when we crossed the finish line, he was kind enough to say, with dry wit, "Look at all those people behind us." In fact, we were the caboose.

In the condo building, where I lived in Albuquerque, I was active in the homeowners association, both as a member and eventually as president of the organization. This service kept me in touch with other people living in the same building.

I also joined the National Federation of the Blind.

In reaching out to the community, I served on the board of directors of local chapters of such organizations as Goodwill Industries, Crime Stoppers of Albuquerque, the Better Business Bureau, the Albuquerque Chamber of Commerce, and the University of New Mexico Cancer Center.

All of these activities not only allowed me to meet other people in the community and work on common causes with them, but they also allowed me to contribute my time and effort to helping others. My own personal problems and concerns often fade into the background when I am doing things that help others and the community.

All of this social interaction led me to run for mayor of Albuquerque in 1993. The mayor's race was non-partisan in that political parties did not openly sponsor any candidate. In the race I entered, there were eleven candidates, including a former governor, two attorneys, several Albuquerque city-council members, a state senator, a former Albuquerque mayor, and a number of other high-profile individuals. I planned to project a vision for the city's future, get a campaign staff functioning, and hit the campaign trail. Over seventy-five thousand votes were anticipated in the race. The top two vote getters would vie in the run-off election.

In those days it was not a media dominated campaign. As mayoral candidates, we all used a more personal approach. We tried to meet as many voters as possible, appear at as many campaign events as we could, and seek media coverage while not relying on it exclusively.

My campaign theme focused on uniting the community to pursue common goals of upgrading roads and public transportation, getting rid of a graffiti epidemic, and introducing measureable quality control of all city services from top to bottom, including more input from the city's rank and file.

As the race neared election day, I received the endorsement of the state's largest newspaper, the *Albuquerque Journal.*

The *Journal's* endorsement pointed to my experience in the broadcast industry and running Commuter Computer in Los Angeles. The endorsement started with the following: "Art Schreiber can't see much across a room, but he can see where Albuquerque is. He may be blind but he can see in detail a better future. And he can see how to get there. The *Journal* recommends Art Schreiber for mayor in the October 3 election."

There also was some mention of my lack of vision by others. On my campaign answering machine there were a few vitriolic comments, such as:

"You dumb bastard, you're blind. How the hell do you think you can run the whole city?"

Another caller suggested, "You know a lot of those city employees won't be working all the time, and you won't be able to see them not working!"

Close to eighty thousand people cast votes in the first election. A young attorney named Martin Chavez received the most votes, followed closely by former New Mexico Governor David Cargo. Martin Chavez (who won the run-off and became mayor) got 14,237 votes in the first election, and I got 9,194 votes, which put me in fifth place, but only 4,277 votes out of the run-off position.

While it was a losing effort for me, I think it was a winning effort for the blind community in Albuquerque, demonstrating a blind person could run a citywide campaign for the city's top office.

After the election, it was time to get back to the real world for me. While I unofficially retired when I left the KOB radio stations and the two other radio stations I managed, I continued to engage in both the workplace and in volunteer activities.

As the year 2003 arrived, a new eyesight calamity had to be addressed. That pinhole of vision that Dr. Jungschaffer had provided me was gradually giving way. That small field of vision was steadily receding.

The loss of my last field of vision was one of the hardest blows I have experienced. At least with that pinhole of vision, there was some visual awareness of the world and the people who live in it. With total loss of vision, a new physical challenge confronted me. Because of experience, I knew that more training was the direction I had to go.

CHAPTER 9
Training Counts

Training is one of the most important things a blind person can do to make independent living a reality. When sight is lost, it is almost automatic to think of training, starting with simple activities like pouring coffee into a cup. Ongoing training efforts as the years pass are just as important. This lesson was brought home to me in a gradual way.

In the late 1980's, Hubbard Broadcasting sold its KOB radio stations, but I stayed on as general manager with two different owners until 1990. By that time, I was sixty-two years old, and it was time to consider a less demanding workload. For a couple of years I managed two other Albuquerque radio stations until I decided to run for mayor of Albuquerque in 1993.

Following that exciting but unsuccessful effort in politics, I did a variety of radio stints that included basketball commentaries after local college games and a two-hour talk show called *The Blind Art Show*. The talk show focused on current issues of interest to people with various disabilities.

At one point, the Commissioners of the New Mexico Commission for the Blind chose me to be chairperson of the Commission. It was a state agency with about eighty employees. After a trial run, I became convinced that I had been in the private sector too long to be suited for full-time government work.

It was toward the end of my six-year stint with *The Blind Art Show* that I began to notice that the lifeline of vision I had in my right eye was diminishing. Where earlier I could see at least one letter at a time on an eye chart, now there was only a blur.

It had been my good fortune since arriving in Albuquerque to be the patient of Dr. Robert W. Reidy, an ophthalmologist with Eye Associates of New Mexico. Dr. Reidy helped me maintain that small field of vision for more than twenty years, both treating and advising me on my eye-care concerns. But by 2003, that small field of vision had gradually faded to the point where I could no longer do basic things like see the printed word, the signature line on a bank check, or the color on a traffic-light signal while walking.

With my sight deterioration in mind, I set aside a six-month period to attend an intensive blind instruction course at the Orientation Center for the New Mexico Commission for the Blind in Alamogordo, New Mexico. When I was head of the Commission that same orientation center was under my jurisdiction. Now, it was I who was under the center's direction.

I moved to a room next to the dormitory at the center and joined a class of about a dozen adult students. At the orientation, I learned we would undergo six months of training, five days a week, eight hours a day. While each student attending had a different eye situation, we all were affected to some degree by impaired vision. To make sure we were prepared to function with no vision at all, we were given sleep shades, which we wore eight hours a day.

During the first few weeks, we hit the basics of how to take care of ourselves. We practiced cooking, cleaning our living quarters, taking care of personal hygiene, handling personal finances, taking care of clothing and shoes, and using electronic devices. We also studied Braille. Every training detail I had learned and used when I had at least some eyesight I now reviewed from the sleep-shade perspective.

We also worked extensively on white-cane mobility, learning how to navigate in a grocery store, in a movie theater, in public transportation, and at public events such as athletic events and symphony performances. We learned how to go up and down stairs and how to navigate in public restrooms.

Much of this I learned to do with limited vision, but now I tackled the same activities with the sleep shade, i.e. no vision at all.

One thing that surprised me then and still surprises me today was a class I took in woodworking. I was trained to operate a power saw and a power sander along with other tools. On one project, I was assigned to make a useful item from scratch. I chose to make a wooden tray with different size compartments to hold personal items such as cuff links, coins, and pens. The tray was made of mahogany, and I still use it to this day. And I still have all my fingers. In jesting with friends, I tell them that had I been younger when I lost my vision, I probably would have considered becoming a neurosurgeon or an airline pilot.

During those six months of training in Alamogordo, we were given only short breaks to leave town. Mostly it was classwork of all kinds, room inspections, and practicing alternative techniques including Braille.

During this time of intense training, I also had some mental adjustments to make. It was frustrating to have to re-learn so many things I had learned before, only to have forgotten them or gotten sloppy in their implementation as years passed.

One misconception I had developed over several years was thinking I could see and operate with that small cone of vision, when in fact it was fading. I did not face up to the changes I needed to make in my daily habits as soon as I should have.

Frustration began to erupt without warning, as it had several times in the past.

During this time, I re-lived an experience I had shortly after I returned to Albuquerque from my seven months of eye surgeries in Los Angeles. I remembered returning to my condo high-rise building one afternoon, intending to go to my unit on the fifteenth floor. I got on the elevator, but instead of pushing the button marked fifteen, I mistakenly pushed a button for some other floor without realizing it.

When I got off the elevator on the wrong floor, it did not occur to me that I was not on the fifteenth floor. I walked to what I thought was my unit and tried my key in the door. It didn't work. I jiggled the doorknob. The noise did alert a resident inside the unit that some unknown person was trying to get in the door. "Who's there? What are you trying to do?" came a loud, challenging voice.

Perhaps I was tired at the end of a workday. For whatever reason life seemed so impossible. I sat down on the carpet in front of the wrong door and started crying, uncontrollably. It took me some time to get myself together. No one ever came out to see what was going on in the hallway.

Finally, I picked myself up, returned to the elevator, focused on my training of how to find the right elevator-floor button, and returned to my own condo. As usual, when I broke down, I was personally humiliated. I was lucky no one came out in the hall while I sat there crying.

Following my six-month stay in Alamogordo, I returned to Albuquerque for a short stay to get re-acquainted with my network of friends and business associates. Then it was off to another training session, this time at a United States Veteran's Administration Blind Rehabilitation Center run program in Tucson, Arizona. The program I attended focused on using technology to assist the blind in daily living. Much of the training time was spent learning how to use computers and other electronic devices.

Some of the new technologies that have come forward in the past thirty years I have tried and discarded, in favor of some more elementary ways of doing things.

I am a fan of an item I refer to as a raised dot. These are small stick-on adhesives about the size of a fingernail. They may have a tiny dot, or a line, or a square on the top side and adhesive on the bottom side. I place these raised dots on all sorts of things, from vitamin bottles to computer keys. They can be an anchor guide for the tip of your finger, as well as a marker. On the computer, for instance, I have a dot on the delete button. That way I am sure I know which button that is, before I delete some message or work. On vitamin bottles, one vitamin bottle may have one round dot. Another vitamin bottle is identified with two round dots. It does take a good memory to stay up with all of them.

Two other training mainstays that are associated with the blind community include guide dogs and Braille. Those are excellent systems and have helped untold numbers of people. I have not chosen either of those methods for my own lifestyle. I tried learning Braille on at least two occasions and made only minor progress. I am a Braille dropout and not proud of it. Before I die, however, I am going to learn it. Other people I know are expert at reading and writing Braille and can do so many practical things using that skill.

Guide dogs also are wonderful for many people. My own lifestyle was not easily compatible with day-to-day maintenance of a dog in my home or while traveling.

However, many people benefit from guide dogs not only for mobility but for companionship as well. As previously reported, my main mobility approach is to use a long white cane, team up with friends and family, and use public transportation.

I confess that after losing my final field of vision, it has been difficult. Nevertheless, I continue to train and practice. As a result, my lifestyle has changed very little.

My life continues to be exciting and rewarding, especially the times I am able to serve others who are just beginning their new life journey without sight.

CHAPTER 10
When Things Go Wrong

Committing to the mobile, independent lifestyle that almost everyone with normal eyesight takes for granted can engage a blind person in some bizarre episodes. I have had my share, and I am sure that all persons who have lost their vision can equally attest.

One of my most memorable events was the fall into the six-foot-deep construction trench across the street from the cleaners. But that was only the beginning. When these unusual incidents happen, they often are personally humiliating. Most of the ones I experienced and from which I escaped without injury, I can now look back on and have a good laugh.

On one occasion, I was walking from my condo to a health club in downtown Albuquerque where I worked out. When I arrived at Fourth Street, there was some construction work underway to build a pedestrian mall. I was walking east on Copper Street. Knowing of the construction from previous trips, I detoured to cross Copper Street from the north side, walking south to avoid the construction. As I stepped off the street curb using my white cane, I detected a large object to my left. By the tap of the cane tip, I realized there was something like a large metallic wall there. I halted, trying to figure out what it was. I raised my white cane tip upward and tapped onto what sounded like some kind of plastic or glass. I couldn't figure out what that was either. Whatever the object was it towered above me. After pausing for a moment, I determined there was no traffic noise on Copper at that moment, so I continued to walk south. About the time I reached the middle of the street, there was a sudden rush of wind, the roar of a big engine, and the swishing sound of a huge vehicle passing within two or three feet of where I was standing. I nearly jumped out of my gym suit and tennis shoes.

It took me a moment to regain my bearings and make it to the far side of Copper. Putting it all together, I realized that the metal wall I tapped was the lower portion of the front end of a bus and the plastic sound was from my cane tapping the bus windshield. At least the bus driver waited until I cleared the traffic lane before roaring away. I took a deep breath and walked on to the health club.

That bus incident happened in an area I knew well. When I traveled to different locales, I was even more likely to make some miscues. On one trip to Florida, I stayed briefly with a good friend whose wife was on a short trip to Europe. They had an upscale home that was shaped like a horseshoe with a large swimming pool in the middle. The master bedroom was on one side of the pool and my guest bedroom was on the opposite side of the pool. A kitchen and den area were in the middle. I awoke early the first morning and decided to go to the kitchen, make some coffee, and then sit out by the pool to enjoy the cool morning air. After getting dressed, I went out the French doors that led from my room to poolside and headed for the kitchen. Somehow, possibly by changing direction to avoid some poolside tables and chairs, I lost my sense of direction. At one point, I decided to turn around and return to my guest room door to get my bearings. As I started to turn, I took a step backward. That was probably the best backward cannonball dive into a swimming pool I have ever made. I never did figure out how I got so close to the edge of the swimming pool without realizing it. That unexpected fall did injure my right leg, but the hurt went away after a few days.

Usually, mishaps occur suddenly and take you by complete surprise.

Close calls with automobiles also can happen unexpectedly. Once while practicing with my long white cane, I stepped off the curb at a street intersection, and a car turning right ran over the end of my cane. It was a close call. Because of that near miss, I called my trainer Jose Sanchez and talked to him about it. He suggested we go on a training exercise, so he could observe how I was crossing street intersections to determine if he could make any recommendations. With Jose observing, I made several crossings at a busy street intersection. After two crossings, he spotted the problem: It was the way I was holding my cane. As I reached an intersection intending to cross, I was holding the cane too close to my body and too vertical. As a result a driver coming from my left couldn't see the cane extending into the street soon enough to slow down or stop. Once I developed a longer reach with the cane into the street, before I actually stepped off the curb, the problem was corrected. My cane has not been hit since I made that adjustment.

Several years later, I was struck by a car but not because of the way I was holding my cane. On that day, I was walking to work on a residential street. At a certain point, I heard a large truck making a loud noise, and it drew my attention. I thought it was a garbage truck on the other side of the street. At that same moment, a woman was backing out of her garage from my right and crossing the sidewalk directly in front of me. I carry my cane in my left hand since I am left handed, and I had my brief case in my right hand. The back of her car slammed into my brief case and knocked me sprawling to the ground, sending my brief case and cane flying. Fortunately, the woman either heard the collision or saw me go down, and she slammed on her brakes. I quickly realized I was not injured, and I got up, reached around, and found both my brief case and cane. The woman remained seated in her car, but she was so shocked at what happened that she started screaming. I walked to the driver's side door and assured her that I was not injured and that I did not hear her car coming due to the noise of the truck across the street. She was so concerned that she might have hurt me that it took her some time to calm down.

Another time I almost checked out happened when I was starting to cross an intersection that did not have traffic lights. As I stepped off the curb to cross, I heard car brakes screech and a horn sound full blast. We are trained to listen for traffic noise. In that case, until the horn and brakes sounded I had heard nothing. The oncoming car was a hybrid a witness told me. Some hybrids are so quiet they cannot be heard if they are not moving at a fast speed. In this case, the hybrid driver braked, honked his horn, and swerved out into an oncoming traffic lane to avoid me. It was a close call. The driver did not stop to say hello.

Another embarrassing incident, although not involving an automobile, occurred on a trip I made to Denver. In the company of Fred Schroeder, his wife Cathy Schroeder, and Sue Benbow, I went into a top-of-the-line men's clothing store. Fred wanted to look for a suit. While Fred, Cathy, and Sue were in the suit department, I wandered to another section of the store close by. There I noted a tall mannequin placed in front of a glass counter. It was dressed in a man's suit and had on a hat. For some whimsical reason, I went up to the mannequin and after standing by it for a brief moment, I reached up with my hand and pulled the front of the hat down over the mannequin's eyes and nose. Suddenly the mannequin moved and said, "What the hell do you think you're doing?" As it walked away, a volley of curse words came back in my direction. What I thought was a mannequin turned out to be a live man, and he did not appreciate my pulling his hat down over his eyes. Sue described what was happening to Fred and Cathy and added at the end, "Fred, the mannequin is walking away!" while dying laughing. I was embarrassed.

Several years later, I didn't do much better at an Albuquerque restaurant. It was a nice, cool day, and the door of the restaurant was being held open by a man who was almost my height. As I awaited a friend to join me in leaving, I hesitated next to the door holder and struck up a conversation with the man, with me doing all the talking. When my friend arrived, she asked me to whom I was talking. It was then she told me that the man holding the door was a wooden statue dressed like an early frontier American Indian.

There are other times I have slipped and fallen on ice, stepped off curbs and steps unknowingly, fallen over furniture, walked into people, and poured liquid from a container that landed on my shoes instead of in the empty glass that was my target.

Through it all I endure, sometimes laughing and sometimes crying.

Out of Sight: Blind and Doing All Right

CHAPTER 11
So Much Remains

I lived my first forty-two years with almost full eyesight. For the next twelve years, I had full sight in one eye only. During the next twenty-eight years, I had limited eyesight—a cone of vision in my right eye that was like looking through a drinking straw. I have lived the last three years with no eyesight at all, perceiving only light and dark with a few vague shadows.

It would be a reportable miracle should I recover any eyesight at all during the rest of my life. I do not understand that to be my destiny. Fortunately, there are miraculous things that remain in a person's life following the loss of vision. Consider:

• Life

- Faith and hope

- Fresh air

- Clean water

- Sufficient food and clothing

- Good health, medical, and dental care

- Family and friends

- Home

- The ability to help other people

- The ability and opportunity to work

- The good fortune to live in a country that values individual freedoms, including freedom of speech and freedom of religion.

I list these items to show that even though blindness is a major loss, most of the basics for a fulfilling, productive, and satisfying life remain. When eyesight is lost, it is natural to feel initially that all is lost, that life itself is over, that nothing remains.

So often anger is the first dominate emotion that engulfs a person. There is anger that sight is lost; there is anger and frustration that the things a person has always done routinely can no longer be done in the same way.

As someone whose initial self-evaluation was "I can't do anything," I was able to continue my career in radio broadcasting. I was able to live independently. I was able to participate in numerous civic activities ranging from the Albuquerque Chamber of Commerce to the local United Way. I was able to serve in organizations and agencies that serve the blind community. I was able to make a credible run for mayor of the City of Albuquerque. I was able to remain active in athletic activities and physical workouts. Most of all, I have been able to assist individuals, on an informal one-on-one basis, who are faced with the same eyesight loss that I experience.

I claim no special talents, no special skills, no special advantages, and no special intelligence or wisdom that allow me to keep going in life after my eyesight failed. I have been blessed by the help of other people, including family and friends over a long, long time as I travel life's journey without sight. Some of that assistance has been noted in this book. There are many untold stories of people who have helped me unselfishly a thousand times in a thousand small ways, and I am grateful to each and every one of them.

Recently, as I stood at an airline ticket counter in Dallas, a man I did not know asked me if he could carry my take-on bag, since he was on the same flight.

He accompanied me all the way to my assigned seat on the plane and put my bag in the overhead storage.

There are those persons who are thoughtful enough to introduce themselves without prompting when they approach me and then tell me when they are leaving.

There are those who are kind enough to offer me their arm or invite me to place my hand on their shoulder as we make our way through an area jammed with people.

Some people are kind enough to call and offer me a ride to and from a meeting that we both are attending.

And bless the people in public restrooms who give you direction to find the paper towel dispenser. Try finding those things in a strange place with your eyes closed.

I have a special recollection of support I received from television producer Ernest Chambers and his wife Veronica Chambers in Los Angeles. They were close friends to my wife Alice and me. During one of my eye surgery recoveries in 1969, Alice's mother died. I was not able to travel, and the funeral was in Pittsburgh. Alice and I discussed the situation, and I told her she needed to go to the service. She said she would never feel right, leaving me at such a critical time. The only way I could persuade her to go was to assure her that Ernie and Veronica would provide daily backup for me while she was away. Only with that assurance was she agreeable to going, and the Chambers did provide that backup, as I knew they would.

The same two friends were with me for most of my vacation twelve years later in Northern New Mexico when my second eye failed, but they departed one day before my vision was lost.

For various reasons, I receive telephone calls and other inquiries on a regular basis from people who are threatened with loss of vision or who have lost their vision. The anguish and anxiety they feel when their vision is threatened or lost is devastating, as it was to me.

When we first talk one-on-one about what has happened to them and what lies ahead, I often perceive they do not hear what I am saying. The shock of their loss of sight is almost too difficult and overwhelming for them to bear, as it was for me.

Often we meet on multiple occasions. My counsel stays pragmatic. Life is not over, so much remains. Following loss of vision, many things a person used to do can still be done if alternate techniques are learned and practiced, aided by assistive technologies.

Training is an essential ingredient; it is available and affordable through such organizations as the National Federation of the Blind, state commissions for the blind in almost two dozen states, many similar government agencies, and through a myriad of other private non-profit organizations.

As in any endeavor, practice counts. Failures and awkward occurrences are part of the process. It is no different from a game of golf. Even professional golfers sometimes send their shots into a sand trap, or into the rough. (By the way, there are blind golfers.)

I am blind, and I accept the fact that my life is different than it would have been had I retained my eyesight. But so much of life remains. I am thankful each day for those things mentioned at the beginning of this chapter. I am hopeful that the experiences told in this book will provide hope to those whose sight is failing or gone, and who have the faith, the courage, and the hope to carry on each day with their new life: *Out of Sight, Blind, and Doing All Right.*

AFTERWORD

"The interesting thing about Art Schreiber is that his employer realized Art's value to the company didn't change that much when Art's vision became impaired."

This opinion was voiced by Fred Schroeder, a longtime friend of Art's and at this writing the first vice president of the National Federation of the Blind.

"When sight is lost or substantially impaired, it is common for many people around you to assume your career is over," Schroeder said in an interview. "Yet often nearly all of your career skills and talents remain. Typically, only a degree of vision is lost. Art Schreiber's ability to manage a team of people running two major radio stations was not lost when his vision became impaired. Art's ability to make business decisions day-by-day was not impaired. Art's knowledge of things like radio programming and advertising strategies was not impaired. Art's social contacts, business contacts, and government contacts were not impaired. Art's ability to make personnel decisions was not impaired," Schroeder said.

Art says that when he thinks about his blind odyssey over three decades, he credits Stan and Karen Hubbard with sticking with him at that crucial time when the shock of lost vision was at its peak. He credits the National Federation of the Blind and Fred Schroeder for showing him the right direction to take to keep his career on track and adjust his lifestyle to new realities.

Over time, Art says he sensed that when sight is lost, many onlookers think a blind person's usefulness in life and ability to function in a normal way is finished—it's over. And it's not only many onlookers who assume this attitude. The person who loses his or her vision often thinks the same thing, he says.

Art often recalls his first training session after losing vision in his second eye, involving the coffee cup and the Ping-Pong ball. His trainer's first question was "What can you do?" His first answer was "I can't do anything."

His road back started in earnest at the first meeting he attended with Fred Schroeder and with Sue Benbow, at the National Federation of the Blind's chapter meeting in Albuquerque. The people at that meeting were friendly, normal people, Art says. "They were doing all right, and they were interested in helping me adjust to new realities. They were willing to share their experiences and knowledge, and they were willing to spend time helping me do the same. They didn't understate the difficulties, but they didn't overstate or dramatize the difficulties, either. If those are the kind of people who are members of the National Federation of the Blind, I want to be one of them," he remembers telling himself.

Based on his long experience working with blind persons, Schroeder says,

"Often it is another person or a group of people who inspire you. When Art joined the local chapter in Albuquerque, we encouraged him to learn, train, and persevere. But he also inspired us. He held a high profile position in Albuquerque as general manager of two of the state's top radio stations, and he was active in civic organizations of all kinds. It was evident early on that he had broken the mind-set that 'If you can't see it, you can't do it.' That attitude is a public misconception about blind people."

"Art's activities and career inspired a number of blind people in Albuquerque who realized what could be done despite the loss of vision," Schroeder said. "And it was an example to other employers who saw firsthand how effective a blind radio station manager could be."

The National Federation of the Blind sums up one of its positions on blindness as follows: "The real problem of blindness is not the lack of eyesight. The real problem is the misunderstanding and lack of information. If a blind person has proper training and opportunity, blindness is only a physical nuisance."

The founder of the National Federation of the Blind was Dr. Jacobus tenBroek, a professor, lawyer, and constitutional scholar, who saw in 1940 that the blind community in the United States needed to unite for collective action on many issues. The organization started in Pennsylvania and eventually moved its national headquarters to Baltimore, Maryland, where it is located today. There are about fifty thousand members. Each state has an affiliate structure at the state level and one or more chapters in different cities within the state.

A national convention is held annually with about twenty-five hundred to three thousand members attending.

The array of services offered by the National Federation of the Blind to people with limited vision is formidable.

A few examples listed on the National Federation of the Blind website at www.nfb.org include the following:

Resources for Living provides listings of information and support for people with limited vision that are available in each state.

Resources for Working gives direction on how a person with limited vision can find a job and how they can contact other people with limited vision who share the same interests in employment, such as law, farming, education, and business operations. Also listed is the latest technology that helps people with limited vision.

Resources for Learning includes instruction on how people with limited vision can study and learn sciences, technology, engineering, and math. It also gives guidance on how to stay up with the news of the day and current events through *NFB-Newsline*. *NFB-Newsline* is for people who wish to get newspaper content on a daily basis, including access to the *New York Times*, *USA Today*, *Wall Street Journal*, and other nationally circulated newspapers. Over three hundred newspapers and magazines are included in the service.

Anyone who cannot read a standard newspaper due to limited vision may qualify for free service.

Resources for Recreation gives guidance to the visually impaired for enjoying all kinds of entertainment including sports activities, performing arts, and staying in good physical condition.

Just about any subject related to blindness can be found under the "Topic Index" on the www.nfb.org website.

The National Federation of the Blind works at both the national level and the state level in support of legislation to even the playing field for people with impaired vision.

The organization is constantly evaluating, testing, and promoting technological advances that aid the blind.

"Once I became a member of the National Federation of the Blind at the local level," Art says, "I also started playing a role at the national level, mainly in the areas of fund-raising and public relations. My personal contacts with high-level radio broadcasters with four major national radio networks also helped spread the word through public service announcements about training services offered to blind people throughout the country."

In 2013, the National Federation of the Blind presented to Art Schreiber the Jacobus tenBroek Award at the national convention in Orlando, Florida, Schroeder said.

The plaque presented reads "Jacobus tenBroek Award, National Federation of the Blind, presented to Arthur Schreiber for your dedication, sacrifice, and commitment on behalf of the blind of this nation. Your contribution is measured not in steps but in miles, not by individual experiences but by your impact on the lives of the blind of the nation. Whenever we have asked, you have answered. We call you our colleague with respect. We call you our friend with love."

Out of Sight: Blind and Doing All Right

About the Author

Arthur A. Schreiber was eight years old and living on an Ohio farm when he first began listening to the radio. He promised himself that one day that voice coming over the airwaves would be his voice. He kept the promise. By 1982, the year he lost his sight, Art was a seasoned broadcast newsman and had interviewed many high-profile newsmakers, including John F. Kennedy, Dr. Martin Luther King, Jr. and the Beatles. He also managed some of the top radio broadcasting operations in America. Despite losing his sight, Art continued managing radio broadcast stations, including KOB-AM and KOB-FM, in Albuquerque New Mexico. He maintained an active role in his community, becoming a civic leader, a candidate for mayor, and a dedicated member of the National Federation of the Blind. Art's refusal to fold his tent when his eyesight failed and his struggle to live life to the fullest will inspire any person who reads his story.

CPSIA information can be obtained at www.ICGtesting.com
Printed in the USA
LVOW10s0745160315

430715LV00030B/835/P